Cyberpoetry & Cyberhumor
Poetry, Humor, Fictrion & 80s Nostalgia

By Edgar G. Allegre

UNIX is a registered trademark of The Open Group

Computer language is a new form of human communication

PREFACE

Imagine the following scenario: It's the year 2010 and UNIX and Linux are the operating systems used by 99% of the Fortune 500 companies. In Stockholm, the Literature Nobel Prize was, for the first time, awarded to a UNIX poet. In London, the famous auctioneer house of Sotheby's reported today that the highest total of any single art sale was paid for a collection of paintings by UNIX Artist. In Burbank, California, the CEO of ABC Network revealed at the stockholders annual meeting that the soap opera, "The UNIX Lab", is the TV show with the highest rating. He added that he has equally high expectations for their new shows: "The UNIX-Dating Game" and "UNIX-Jeopardy". In Madison Avenue, advertising agencies are discovering that the best vehicle for their ads are UNIX terminals. According to "The Journal of Advertising" the messages displayed on UNIX screens after the user logs in, have the highest rate of awareness of any advertising medium. In Boston, Harvard became the first university to offer a major in "Psychology & Sociology of the UNIX User". And this month's People Magazine covers all about the latest rage: UNIX Psychotherapy.

If you think all this sounds too farfetched, then welcome to "Cyberpoetry & Cyberhumor", where UNIX is nothing less than a new form of human communication, the electronic age Esperanto of the XXI Century.

UNIX DOES
LUNCH
WITH
BURBANK
TV PRODUCERS

FROM THE MINDS OF THE PRODUCERS OF "GENERAL HOSPITAL" COMES THE SOAP OPERA FOR THE 21ST CENTURY:"THE UNIX LAB" WITH JESSICA ALBA, THE EVIL SYSTEM ADMINISTRATOR

"THE UNIX LAB" EPISODE 111.
RANDOLPH RASTER'S DEEP SET EYES SCAN THE EMPTY UNIX LAB.
BEING SOMEWHAT PSYCHIC, HE HAS THE STRONG SUSPICION THAT
THERE'S A USERS' GROUP PARTY THAT HE WASN'T INVITED TO.
HE PROCEEDS TO LOG IN.

login: randolph
Password:

News: See you at you know where and you know when.
Don' t anybody tell you know who.

```
    $ write pat
    pat is not logged in.
    $ write bret
    bret is not logged in.
    $ write steve
    steve is not logged in.
    $ write donna
    donna is not logged in.
    $ write toni
    toni is not logged in.
    $ write rob
    rob is not logged in.
    $ write john
    john is not logged in.
    $ write marcia
    marcia is not logged in.
    $ write james
    james is not logged in.
    $ write rod
    rod is not logged in.
    $ write mark
    mark is not logged in.
    $ write anybody !!!
    nobody logged in but you know who !!!
    $
```

UNIX'S CELEBRITY CORNER OF THE 80s

EDDIE MURPHY LOGGING IN

login: Eddie
Password:
You gotta be jiving me, man! That ain't your password:
login:

GARY COLEMAN LOGGING IN

login: Gary
Password:
WHAT YOU TALK'NG ABOUT!!
login:

MICHAEL JACKSON LOGGING IN (CIRCA HIS "JACKSON FIVE" DAYS)

login. mj
Password:
A-B-C/lo-gin wrong/try again/don't take long
login:

MICHAEL JACKSON LOGGING IN (CIRCA HIS "THRILLER" ALBUM)

login: Michael
Password:
You're not the gloved one
login:

MICHAEL JACKSON LOGGING IN (CIRCA HIS "MOONWALKER" ALBUM)

login: Michael
Password:
You're not the Man in the Mirror
login:

4

PLACIDO DOMINGO LOGGING IN

login: Placido
Password:
FI-I-IGARO-O-O-O NO!
login.

PORKY PIG LOGGING OUT

$ logout
T-T-THAT'S ALL FOLKS
login:

BUGS BUNNY LOGGING IN

login: bugs
Password:
WHAT'S UP DOC
$

JOHNNY CARSON LOGGING IN

login: Johnny
Password:
He-eeree-es-Johnny

AND ON THE 7TH DAY, GOD FORGOT HIS PASSWORD

login:
password:
Login incorrect
login:

80s MADONNA LOGGING IN

```
login:
Password:
Who's that girl?
```

CHEECH CHANGING HIS PROMPT

```
$ PS1=Quepasa
Quepasa
```

CINDY LAUPER SETTING THE TIME

```
$ date
Time after Time EST
```

WOODY ALLEN'S COMPUTER

```
$ whoami
Have you been skipping your therapy again?
$
```

POST-SCANDAL IVAN BOESKY

```
$ PS1=   ¢
```

**UNIX USERS
KNOW THAT
A LOT
OF $PATHS
LEAD TO ROME**

```
login: eltonjohn
Password:

$ echo $PATH
The Yellow Brick Road
$
```

```
login: thebeatles
Password:

$ echo $PATH
The Long and Winding Road
$login: ledzepellin
password:

$  echo $PATH
Stairway to Heaven
$
```

```
login: robertfrost
password

$ echo $PATH
The Road Not Taken
```

$HOME
SWEET
$HOME

UNIX IN MALIBU, CALIFORNIA

```
$  echo ~/
/Beachfront/HOME/
$
```

UNIX ON A CENTURY 21 TERMINAL

```
$  echo ~/
/HOME/sold/
$
```

UNIX IN PLEASANT HILL, CALIFORNIA

```
$  echo ~/
/HOME/Sweet/Home
$
```

UNIX IN NEW YORK CITY

```
$  echo ~/
/247East/22ndStreet/Forty - thirdFloor
$
```

UNIX IN THE EXECUTIVE WING

```
$  echo ~/
/WhiteHouse/HOME/
$
```

UNIX IN THE HEART OF AMERICA

```
$  echo ~/
/HOME/of the Brave/Land/of theFree
$
```

UNIX DURING THE WORLD SERIES

```
$  echo ~/
/first/second/third/HOMERUN
4
```

UNIX IN BONANZA

```
$  echo ~/
/LaPonderosa
$
```

UNIX
&
THE
BEATLES

THE UNIX VERSION OF " HEY, WAIT A MINUTE MR. POSTMAN "

```
$  mail
No mail
$  Hey, wait a minute Mr. /usr/mail ! !
```

WHAT HOLLYWOOD CELEB WOULD YOU CHOOSE AS YOUR SYSTEM ADMINISTRATOR?

PAT SAJAK
ALEX TREBEK

**WHAT IF PAT SAJAK OF THE "PRICE IS RIGHT"
WERE THE SYSTEM ADMINISTRATOR?**

login: johndoe
Password:

Are you ready to buy some vowels & consonants?

```
UN  X  SyS  em  V  Re  ea  e  3.1
Cop  ri  ht  (c)  1987 AT &

Y u  hav  all

$ su
# /etc/wall "T   sys ill  e  own for  ftw  i
s  a ll  ion  rom  6:00  o  7:00 p.  to i  ht."
#
```

WHAT IF ALEX TREBEK OF "JEOPARDY" WERE THE SYSTEM ADMINISTRATOR?

What is login: johndoe
What is Password:

What Is today's banner & news: The system will be down from 6:30 to 7:30 P.M.

```
$ su
# /etc/wall "At 60,000 words and 154 main senses,
it is the longest entry in the The Oxford English
Dictionary"
# sleep 16000
# /etc/wall "What is the verb set"
#
```

UNIX
GOES TO
THE
"DATING GAME"

**HOW DO THE PRODUCERS OF "THE DATING GAME" MATCH
CONTESTANTS? VERY EASILY WITH UNIX!**

```
$  diff contestant1 contestant2
$
```

UNIX
TURNS
INTO A
TREKIE

LIGHT YEARS FROM THE MILKY WAY. UNIX IS ONE MORE PASSENGER ABOARD THE STARSHIP ENTERPRISE

```
login: captain
Password:

Materialize yourself for Cosmo-Monopoly at 19:30
tonight in the Nuclear Engine Room.

# /usr/lib/reject -r "Prlnter down.  Cosmlc Law
states that the magnetlc fleld generated by Planet
Tltanus-Unlx's orblt alters the escape sequences
of our lazer printer resulting in a
nonproportlonal font kerning/font pitch ratio."
STARPRINTER
destlnatlon "STARPRINTER" is no longer accepting
requests.
#
```

**HAVE YOU EVER
WONDERED WHY
THE MENUS AT
SILICON VALLEY
RESTAURANTS
LOOK LIKE ENTRIES
FROM THE
ONLINE MANUAL?**

```
$ man lunch
LUNCH(1)   UNIX Prograrnmer's Manual   LUNCH(1)
```

NAME
        Hacker"s lunch

SYNOPSIS
        lunch [look under description for menu of the day]

DESCRIPTION
Hexadecimal Oyster Cocktail -- F oysters in their Bourne
                Shell flled in 1 MB of avocado sauce.
Binary Soup -- Like alphabet soup but with only 0´s & 1´s
Motorola 30836 Sirloin Steak -- A steak wlth 30836 calories!
                Comes wlth perfect hash browns
$HOME - made Apple Pie
Floating polnt merlngue Island

And a cholce of one of the followlng:

Jlm Blinn B-splined Hot Tea
        or
Stroustrup drink -- served in a C shaped glass
        or
Encrypted drink -- a mysterious combination of
    exotic beverages!

NOTE
        $15.95

UNIX
AS A
FARMHAND

SOMEWHERE IN THE BACKROADS OF TENNESSEE

login: OldMcDonald
Password:

```
$ who
Old McDonald had a farm,
And on hIs farm.
He had two Macintoshes
And three Sun Workstations
And now he's gettIng a couple of supercomputers.
Old McDonald had a farm,
Now he has a computer lab.
Old McDonald has a lab.
Ee-ya-a ee-ya-a Oooo-oooo
$
```

THE UNIX THEORY
OF THE
CONCEPTION
OF THE
UNIVERSE

THIS IS THE WAY UNIX THEORY EXPLAINS THE CREATION
OF THE UNIVERSE


```
$ at Big Bang    <    Creatlon.of.Universe
job 0.a   at   one day billions of years ago
$
```

CRO-MAGNON, UGAUGALOOP: THE FIRST UNIX USER

CRO-MAGNON, UGAUGALOOP'S UNIX ENVIRONMENT VARIABLES

```
$ printenv
HOME=Stoneageland
SHELL=Prehistoric
PATH=hang a left after the Tyrannosaur's fossil and go straight
till you hit the volcanoes (watch out for the candent lava: it's
really hot!), third cave from the top, grunt before entering
TERM=B.C. IBM compatible
USER=ugaugaloop
TZ=Sundial
$
```

UNIX
GOES
WAY
BACK

CRO-MAGNON UGAUGALOOP IS GENERALLY CREDITED AS BEING THE DISCOVERER OF THE INFINITE LOOP CONCEPT CIRCA 33.000 B.C.

logIn: ugaugaloop
Password:

News for Cro-Magnons: Tyrannosaurus Rex huntIng season to start tomorrow.

```
$ bc
s=VI
whIle ( s == MV) (
        s
        s =- 1
)
V
IV
III
II
I
0
- I
- II
- III
(etc.)
```

B.C. UNIX

THE ROMAN EMPEROR JULIUS CEASAR INVOKES THE
ARBITRARY PRECISION DESK-CALCULATOR LANGUAGE.
HAIL B.C.!


```
$ bc
III + IV
VII
( I + II ) *X
XXX
scale=3
I/II
0.V00
```

UNIX
MAIL FORWARDING
&
THE ROMAN SENATE

ACCORDING TO HISTORICAL RECORDS, IN THE YEAR 44 B. C.,
JULIUS CAESAR WAS ASSASSINATED IN THE ROMAN
SENATE BY BRUTUS AND OTHER CONSPIRATORS.
THAT SAME YEAR HIS UNIX MAIL WAS FORWARDED.

```
$ mail -F caesar
Forwarding to brutus
$
```

UNIX
MAIL FORWARDING
&
THE COURT OF HENRY VIII

EVEN WITH THE MAIL FORWARDING COMMAND IT WASN'T EASY KEEPING UP HENRY VIII, KING OF ENGLAND, WHO MARRIED A TOTAL OF SIX TIMES.

```
$ mail -F catherine.of.aragon
Forwarding to anne.boleyn
$ mail -F anne.boleyn
Forwarding to jane.seymur
$ mail -F jane.seymour
Forwarding to anne.of.cleves
$ mail -F anne.of.cleves
Forwarding to catherine.howard
$mail -F catherine.howard
Forwarding to catherine.parr
```

THE
UNIX
PALETTE

THE UNIX PALETTE ACCORDING TO POP ART LEGEND ANDY WARHOL

```
login: andy
Password:


$ setcolor Campbell Soup red   Mao Tse-Tung yellow
$
```


THE UNIX PALETTE ACCORDING TO VAN GOGH

```
login: vangogh
Password:


$ setcolor pulsating yellow   scintillating violet
$
```

THE UNIX PALETTE ACCORDING TO DALI

login: dali
Password:

I ♥ Gala!

```
$ setcolor Gala rose   Gala blue
$
```

THE UNIX PALETTE ACCORDING TO POP SINGER PRINCE

login: prInce
Password:

Your Royal Badness!

```
$ setcolor purple rain    red corvette
$
```

THE UNIX PALETTE ACCORDING TO ABSTRACT PAINTER, VASILY KANDINSKY

login: vasily
Password:

There Is no must in art because art is free.

$ setcolor abstract blue   dot red

$

ABSTRACT ART
FINDS
A NEW EXPONENT
IN
UNIX

VASILI KANDINSKI III COMBINES ABSTRACT PAINTING AND UNIX TO CREATE A NEW ART FORM: "ABSTRAUNIXCT"

```
$ su +++++++++++++++++++++ $ df @@@@@@@@@@@@
 ######### $ od  !! !! !! !! !! !!!! !! login:
$ ls -a -a -a -a -a  $ dc   $ sh   $ sleep 3000

^D   WHO AM I    $  wwbinfo    $ yacc
. . . . . . . . . . . . . . . . $$$$$$$$$$$$$$$$$$ !! !! !

$ date                                    $ chown
```

THE UNIX POEM
DEDICATED
TO THAT
FAITHFUL KITCHEN
ASSISTANT:
THE
BLENDER

THE FOR LOOP OF A BLENDER
by
e.e.cunlx


```
$ cat blender
for i
do
    take those red tomatoes
    rlp them apart
    mlx them wlth the peppers
    disjointing them both
    the onions & garlic
    had no other choice
    but to blend in
    fast and for good
    round and around
    all of them go
    screeching to ears
    that pretend to be deaf
    hurrledly orbiting around my shiny stainless steel blade
    till all that's left of them is a thick, yummy sauce!!
done
```

**THE UNIX POET KNOWS OF
THE INTANGIBLE UMBILICAL
CORD THAT LINKS YOUR
OPTICAL MOUSE TO
THE ONE
YOU
LOVE**

OPTIC-MOUSE LOVE
by
Bit Van Map

You're the red guiding light of an optic mouse,
gliding across the inconditional grid of my heart.

THE UNIX POET ALSO
KNOWS OF THE INTANGIBLE
LINE THAT CONNECTS
THE CONCEPT OF
REBOOTING WITH
THE CONCEPT OF LOVE

REBOOTING IS LOVING YOU A LITTLE BIT MORE
by
UNIXMan

Every time I think of you, my system reboots,
magically putting me in your HOME directory.

THE UNIX POET FULLY UNDERSTANDS THAT PERENNIAL ROMANTIC SYMBOL: THE DANGEROUS HACKER

A LOVE FOR HACKER
-- Anonymous

Hacker, hacker,
access freely all my paths,
"vi" into my most intimate files,
and **"more"** my .login script,
or **"ed"** my passwrd flle.
nobody knows me,
as well as you do,
I've sworn I'll wrlte no permissions to bar you,
from being who you are,
a hacker at heart,
roaming my CPU with fondling curiosity,
I can but love your hacking around,
because you know whoami and wherelwannabe,
Hacker, hacker,
"chdir" about,
to the obscure depths of my hierarchlcal system,
till you find that long encrypted love file,
to which I'm positively sure you hold the only
> < key >
> that can decode it!

YOU CAN'T CONSIDER
YOURSELF AN
AVANT-GARDE POET
UNTIL YOU'VE WRITTEN
YOUR FIRST BINARY POEM
& HAD IT PUBLISHED
IN THE NEW YORKER

WHY DO THE GRACES

01101011 101001000 01011001 01000100 01001111
      01010100   01001000   01000101
      01000111   01010010   01000001 0 1000011 01000101 01010011

01110111 01101000 01111001 01100100 01101111 01110100 01101000
01100101
01000111 01110010 01100001 01100011 01100101 01110011
01101110 01101111 01110111
01100100 01100101 01110011 0110010101110010 01110100 01101000
01100101
01001101 01110101 0111110011 01100101 00111111
01010100 01101000 01100101 01111001 01101000 01100001 01110100
01100101
01100010 01110010   01101001 01100111   01101000 01110100
01110010 01101001   01100010 01100010   01101111 01101110 01110011
01110100 01111001   01101001 01101110   01100111 01110111
01101111   01101111   01100100 01100101 01101110

      01110011 01101000 01101111 01100101 01110011
          01010111 01100001 01101100 01110100 01100101
              01001100 01100001 01101110 01100100 01101111

54

MORE
BINARY
POETRY

FLASH. UNIX FAMOUS POET, e.e. cunix, ANNOUNCED, AT
A PRESS CONFERENCE, THAT ALL HIS WRITING FROM
THIS POINT ON, WOULD BE IN BINARY.

01011001
by
e.e.cunlx
01000010010001010010101
01001010001010010101001
10010100010000101001001
11110000101010100100101!!

SOME CRITICS AFFIRM
THAT IT WAS NOT
UNTIL ROBERT FROSTY
FLAKES DISCOVERED UNIX
THAT HIS REAL
POETRY-WRITING
GENIUS
BLOSSOMED

MB OF YOUR LOVE
        by
Robert Frosty Flakes, Version 2.2

For a mg byte of your love
To become a nice --19 process in your cpu
A crypted file in your HOME directory
Your secret password in your /etc/passwd
Or an "alias" that you typed in your login script
Don't kill -9 my love
My love is 1,000,000 dpi
My thoughts run at 1999 mhz to vIsualize you
Don't reset.
I'll be content to be your User's manual
GIve you all the technIcal support you need
If you'll only link my name with yours
$ In you me
Just let me be
More than garbage
In your /usr/tmp

**SOME CRITICS
AFFIRM THAT
HIS OCTAL POEMS
ARE AMONG THE BEST**

An octal poem by UNIX poet Robert Frosty Flakes


```
$ od-c Frost8.8
000LOVE 0DESIRE  000LUST 00STRAW 000PALMS SUNROOF
0PURPLE MASCARA 00TOUCH 00FLUTE  0000SOFT 00HUMID
*
000MELT 00BODY 0000TOP 000SURF  000SKATE   000PINK
00000IN   000OUT 000NTOP 00PIANO  SYMPHONY 000LOVE
```

-- The remainder of Frost8.8 is dumped --

WHEN THE JAPANESE GARDENER MOONLIGHTS WRITING UNIX POETRY

LOGGING AS BAMBOO
by
San-ron-San

Let me humbly login as bamboo ROOT
And sow and edit the seed of love file
In your $HOME directory
So it may flourish there
Like a kamikaze Trojan Horse!

SHAKESPEARE'S
BAUD RATE

SHAKESPEARE'S SONATAS NEVER QUITE READ THE SAME AFTER SOMEBODY MYSTERIOUSLY CHANGED THE BAUD RATE OF HIS PRINTER SCRIPT IN WILLIAM'S /usr/spool/lp/model

PRINTER'S GARBLED OUTPUT AFTER THE SABOTAGE

```
#&%*&*!@#&&*&**((&*%$#@@*&()(*&^%$#@@@@&*((
&*^*)(*%%^%%#$!%^&*#(@#!)^&%$*()$%^&**()($&%^$$
*&^%*$#(!@(%$#@@**&^%$&^#^&*(((($##%@#!*^%$&&&
#$%^%**$#(!@(%$#@@**&^%$%^#^&*(((($##%@!#$%^$^&
&*()()&*^%$%^&*%^$%^%$#@!^&*()(*&^%$#@!#$%^$^$
&*(%$%&*!^$%#&[*!#$%&()^!)&%$#!$*^(&%$# $%&^%*(
#@!^%$%&%)(*^)&%$#"*^&%$#^&%$#*@%@%$^%$#$*^&
&#&%*&*!@#&&*&**((&*%$#@@*&()(*&^%$#@@@@&*((
&*^*)(*%%^%%#$!%^&*#(@#!)^&%$*()$%^&**()($&%^$$
*&^%*$#(!@(%$#@@**&^%$&^#^&*(((($##%@#!*^%$&&&
#$%^%**$#(!@(%$#@@**&^%$%^#^&*(((($##%@!#$%^$^&
&*()()&*^%$%^&*%^$%^%$#@!^&*()(*&^%$#@!#$%^$^$
%$%&*!^$%#&[*!#$%&()^!)&%$#!&*^(&%$# $%&^%*(
^%$%&%)(*^)&%$#"*^&%$#^&%$#*@%@%$^%$#$*^&
```

LEGEND HAS IT THAT AFTER SEEING THE GARBLED OUTPUT, SHAKESPEARE STRONGLY CONSIDERED CHANGING THE SONATA'S TITLE TO "LA GARBLED SONATA", BUT HIS PUBLISHING HOUSE OBJECTED

UNIX
&
THE GIANTS
OF LITERATURE:
WILLIAM
SHAKESPEARE

SHAKESPEARE'S FAVORITE UNIX TOOL WAS THE STYLE ANALYSIS PROGRAM.
LEGEND HAS IT THAT AFTER USING IT TO ANALYZE HIS FAMOUS TRAGEDY " ROMEO AND JULIET " , SHAKESPEARE SOBBED .
"THIS IS A REAL TRAGEDY. I - I - I CAN'T BELIEVE I USED 'THY' 3.5 MORE TIMES THAN I ORIGINALLY INTENDED!"

Style Analysis of "Romeo and Juliet" (1591)

Measure	"Romeo and Juliet"
Number of times the word "thy" is used	112.5
Number of times "ho!" and "ho?" appear	77
Percentage of compound Sentences divided by the number Of times the following expletives Are used: "thou hads't suck'd" , "allck the day ! " or " alas "	8.23%
Percentage of sentences Having one of the following Words: " thee ", " spite " or "fortnight"	18.7%

UNIX
IN
MADISON
AVENUE

A UNIX AD FOR PRUDENTIAL INSURANCE COMPANY

```
$ cat  /user/lib/crontab
#
# Jack & Jill weren't covered by Prudential
#
# min      hour     day      month    day-of-week    event
# (0-59)   (0-23)   (1-31)   (1-12)     (0-6)
# - - - - - - - - - - - - - - - - - - - - - - - - - - - - - - - - - - - - -
10        12       10       7        0             Jack & Jill went up the hill
18        12       10       7        0             To fetch a pale of water
20        12       10       7        0             Jack fell down
21        12       10       7        0             And broke his crown
22        12       10       7        0             And Jill came tumbling after
```

A SPECIAL UNIX
COMMAND RESERVED
FOR
VERY NICE PEOPLE

MARCIE IS SUCH A " VERY NICE " GIRL. THAT INSTEAD OF
USING THE NICE COMMAND, SHE USES THE VERY NICE.


```
$ very nice --19 myjob
$
```

THE
UNIX
CIRCUS

THE UNIX CIRCUS IS IN TOWN AND LATE AT NIGHT IN ONE OF THE CIRCUS' TENTS, SYSTEM ADMINISTRATOR, TONZO THE CLOWN, LOGS IN.

```
login: tonzo
Password:
```

Mandatory seminar for all clowns: "The UNIX method
for getting more laughs out of your jokes". Tuesday 12:00 p.m.
in the Main Tent. Be punctual!

```
# /usr/llb/reject - r  "Printer down . Caesar Domo the elephant
trainer, was teaching Tumbo a new trick: sit on a stool and turn
on the printer. But Tumbo got it backwards. He sat on the printer
and tried to turn on the the stool. Printer down until Fri,
for repairs."   FUNPRINTER
destination  "FUNPRINTER" is no longer accepting requests
#
```

WHEN ELEPHANT TRAINERS ARE FERVENT FANS OF
THE UNIX OPERATING SYSTEM

ONE WEEK AFTER THE PRINTER INCIDENT ,
CEASAR DOMO WAS TEACHING TUMBO A NEW UNIX
TRICK --- HOW TO LOG IN. BUT TUMBO WENT INTO A
FRENZY WHEN SHE REPEATEDLY FAILED TO REMEMBER
HER PASSWORD., SHE SMASHED THE KEYBOARD AND ATE
THE USER'S MANUALS. THE FIRST PART OF THE USER'S
MANUAL THAT TUMBO MUNCHED DOWN WAS THE
FILE - FORMAT SECTION PAGES WHICH DESCRIBE
THE FILE /etc/passwd.

THE UNIX
CORE - OLYMPICS
GAMES,
ONLY THE BEST
WILL BE THERE

**MARCIE STANDS A GOOD CHANCE OF MAKING THE U.S.
CORE - OLYMPICS TEAM. SHE'S BEEN TRAINING VERY HARD.**

```
$ ls - lt
-rw-r--r--    1    marcle          25687601200  Jul 23    24:08   core . 6
-rw-r--r--    1    marcle          22569060000  Jul 23    23:35   core . 5
-rw-r--r--    1    marcle          15977900356  Jul 23    23:23   core . 4
-rw-r--r--    1    marcle            385025891  Jul 23    23:12   core . 3
-rw-r--r--    1    marcle                79620  Jul 23    23:01   core . 2
-rw-r--r--    1    marcle                   94  Jul 23    22:55   core . 1
$
```

**UNIX USER
ADDED
TO LIST
OF
ENDANGERED SPECIES**

ON HIS SECOND DAY ON THE SYSTEM, BEGINNER LEVEL
UNIX USER, BERNIE FIFO LOGS IN TO FIND OUT HE HAS
BEEN PUT ON THE UNIX ENDANGERED SPECIES LIST BY
THE OTHER USERS BECAUSE THE DAY BEFORE HE DECIDED
TO PRACTICE THE /bin/rm COMMAND IN THE OTHER USERS'
DIRECTORIES

login: bernie
Password:

THE UNIX ENDANGERED SPECIES LIST: ONE BERNIE FIFO

$

ANOTHER USE
FOR THE ignoreof
COMMAND WHICH
YOU WON'T
FIND DOCUMENTED
IN THE
USER'S MANUAL

**AFTER TEDDY, OSCAR & RICK DID A NUMBER ON DODIE,
SHE DECIDED TO IGNORE THEM FOR THE REST OF THEIR
NATURAL LIFES**

```
login: dodle
Password:

$ set  ignoreof teddy
$ set  ignoreof oscar
$ set  ignoreof rick
$
```

THE SCIENTIFIC
PROWESSES
OF
UNIX'S
FAVORITE SCHOLAR
DR. VAN VON RAM

UNIX DR. VAN VON RAM OBTAINED A ROCKEFELLER
GRANT FOR BEING THE FIRST PERSON TO wc BOTH THE
DECLARATION OF INDEPENDENCE AND THE BILL OF RIGHTS


```
$ both Declaration Billrights
    12346  21322
$
```


DR. VAN VON RAM WAS ALSO THE FIRST ONE TO COUNT
THE NUMBER OF "OF's" IN THE DECLARATION OF
INDEPENDENCE.
AFTER REALIZING THE VAST NUMBER OF "OF's" IN THE
DECLARATION OF INDEPENDENCE, HE PROPOSED THAT
ITS NAME BE CHANGED TO "THE DECLARATION OF OF".


```
$ grep - c  of  Declaration
1290
$
```

THE ROLE
UNIX'S find
COMMAND
IN THE FBI
** TOP SECRET **
FILES

WHAT BAFFLES HARRY ENIAC'S FBI COLLEAGUES IS THAT
HE CAPTURES CRIMINALS WITHOUT EVER GETTING UP
FROM HIS UNIX WORKSTATION.
QUESTION: HOW DOES HARRY LOCATE CRIMINALS ON
THE "FBI'S MOST WANTED LIST" AND MAKE IT SEEM AS
EASY AS ABC?
ANSWER: WITH THE find COMMAND !


```
login: eniac
Password
Crime doesn't pay  (cash)

$ find  / -name "Cory"  I  find  / -size  "6 feet tall"
I  find  / -weight -  "180 lbs"  I  find  / -race   "euroasiatic"
I  find  / -nickname  "stoneface"
Cory Stoneface" Tsan  ---- Comitting an armed robbery
at 7 - 11 store on the corner of Laguna St and Arroyo Av., CA.
$  find  / -rank  "public enemy no 1"
Loree "Big mammah" Abundah --- 7701 North Ellway
St. Seattle , WA.
$  find  / -rank "public enemy no. 234"
Joe "Trust me" Belamoe --- Interstate 1501 heading
North towards Highway 60
$
```

NOBODY CAN
OUTSMART
A SECRET AGENT
UNIX TERMINAL

login: Agent 008
Password:
Secret password :
Super - Secret password:
Ultra - Secret password:
Super - Ultra - Secret password:
Ultra - Ultra - Secret password:

Login Incorrect
You ' re not Agent 008!
Sending a high voltage electrical discharge to the keyboard!!

login:

UNIX
CLASSIFIEDS

A CLASSIFIED AD IN THE HEART OF TEXAS

$ find "attractive cowgirl" I find "single" I find
"18 - 22 yrs. old " I find "into spurs & high heels" I find
"into saddles & lingerie " I find " into lassoes between
satin sheets " I find " into hot chill & macho men" > (713) 555 44444

UNIX PETS

THE UNIX USER COMPLETE NAME GUIDE FOR PETS

If you have a GOLDFISH name him Floppy
If you have a TROUT in a frying pan name it Cooked Mode
If you have a DALMATIAN name him Bitmap
If you have a PEACOCK name him Hires
If you have a MONARCH BUTERFLY name it RGB
If you have a POLICE DOG name him Byte
If you have a FIERCE POLICE DOG name him Megabyte
If you have a MEAN. BAD PIT BULL name him Baud
If you have a MEANER. BADDER PIT BULL name him Bauder
If you have the MEANEST. BADDEST PIT BULL name him Baudest
If you have a BUG you can call it Bug
If you have a CAN OF INSECTICIDE call it Debug
If you have a TOY POODLE name him Pixel
If you have a TOY TERRIER name him Joystick
If you have a CHIHUAHUA name him Laptop
If you have a DACHSHUND name him Cursor
If you have a BULLDOG name it Block
If you have a PORCUPINE name him Pointer
If you have a MUTT name him Cryptic
If you have a PARROT name him Comment
If you have a PET ROCK name him Constant
If you have a DOLPHIN that has a higher IQ than yours name it CPU
If you have a LITTER of laboratory rats you can call it Database.
(Name the first born FIFO)
If you have a DISK DRIVE you can call it Device
If you have a ANT FARM name it Network
If you have a TERMITE name it Documentation
If you have a BURRO with Moctezuma's revenge name him Dump
If you have a BRANDED HORSE name him Font
(The following are also acceptable options: Helvetica,
Century, Bookman, Optima , Times Roman, Tmes Bold,
American Typewriter, etc .)
If you have a NEW - BORN PUPPY name him Backup
If you have a GREENHOUSE name it Environment
If you have a PET witch hiccups name him Iteration
If you have a STUD name it Formatter
If you have a SADDLE HORSE name him Mount
If you have a WILD HORSE name him Unmount

If   you   have   an AMOEBA name it Fragmentation
If   you   Mother hates your PET it really doesn't matter what you name it .
                            since she'll rename it Glitch
If   you   have   a NARCOTICS DETECTOR DOG name it Grep
If   you   have   a TURTLE name him Hardware
If   you   have   a pair of KISSING FISH name them Interface
If   you   have   a HAMSTER that loves to run in its playwheel
                            name it Loop
If   you   have   an OCTOPUS name it Multitask
If   you   have   a STUMP name it Log
If   you   have   a CARRIER PIGEON name it Modem (or mail)
If   you   have   a MINIATURE SCHNAUZER name it Micro
If   you   have   an ELECTRIC EEL name it Conductor
If   you   have   a THANKSGIVING TURKEY name it Menu
If   you   have   a REEF name it Network
If   you   have   a CARD-COUNTING CHIMPANZEE who counts cards
                            like Dustin Hoffman's character in the movie "Rainman",
                            name him Operator
If   you   have   a GREYHOUND name it Runtime
If   you   have   a INDIAN GREYHOUND name him Guru
If   you   have   a RACEHOURSE name it Priority
If   you   have   a DOG SHOW CHAMPION name it Graphics
If   you   have   a PSYCHOANALIST name him Debug
If   you   have   a DOGSLED TEAM name it Pipeline
If   you   have   a CAT that follows you everywhere name him Lint
If   you   have   a AMPHIBIOUS PET name it Portable
If   you   have   a SIAMESE CAT with big blue eyes name him Raster
If   you   have   to take your dog to TRAINING SCHOOL name
                            him Reformat
If   you   have   a pet so OBEDIENT that you never have to give him
                            an order twice name him RISC
If   you   have   a DOG that keeps you up at nights with his howling
                            name him Zombie
If   you   have   a SNAKE name it Scroll
If   you   have   a DOBERMAN name it Security
If   you   have   a SNAIL name it C Shell (or Bourne Shell or Korn Shell)
If   you   have   a FIREFLY name it LED (or Light Pen)
If   you   have   a MOUSE you can call him Mouse
If   you   have   a DOG that's always chasing his tall name him Wraparound

ASSOCIATION
OF
UNIX
PSYCHOLOGISTS

**WHEN YOU FEEL SO FRUSTRATED BY PRESSURES OF LIFE
THAT YOU THINK YOU'RE ABOUT EXPLODE, IMPLEMENT
THE FOLLOWING UNIX THERAPY.
RECOMMENDED DOSIS: AT LEAST ONCE A WEEK, BUT NOT
MORE THAN TWICE A DAY!!**

```
$ leftlovers > /dev/null
$ dirty laundry > /dev/null
$ dirty dishes > /dev/null
$ unpaid bills > /dev/null
$ estranged loves > /dev/null
$ blue memories > /dev/null
$ rainy days > /dev/null
$ boring job > /dev/null
$ Dolphins lose again > /dev/null
$ yesterday's fashion > /dev/null
$ bad times > /dev/null
$ lousy walters > /dev/null
$ the boss > /dev/null
(Don't you feel like a new person now!)
$
```

THE UNIX INSTITUTE OF
ADVANCED STUDIES REPORTS
THAT THE NUMBER OF CASES
WHERE THE UNIX USER IS
FINALLY ABLE TO LOG IN
AS A SUPERUSER AND
PROCEEDS TO ACT LIKE
A SUPERVILLAIN IS
INCREASING AT AN
ALARMING RATE

**THIS IS THE WAY THE UNIX PSYCHOTHERAPY PROGRAM
WOULD TREAT A PATIENT WITH AN IDENTITY CRISIS**

```
$  whoami
$  whoami
$  whoami
```

SYSTEM SHUTDOWN NOW ! ! !

UNIX
THERAPY
FOR
THE
LONELY HEARTS

CASE IN POINT: IDINA LOVELESSKY WHO IS STARVED FOR A LITTLE AFFECTION

login: idina
Password:

Love is like oxygen, you can't live without it.

```
$  ls
README
$  mv  README LOVEMEPLEASE
$  ls
LOVEMEPLEASE
$
```

HOW TO DEAL
WITH
GRUMPY UNIX
TERMINALS

DR. RAM SMITH, UNIX PSYCHOLOGIST, SAYS THAT UNIX TERMINALS ARE JUST LIKE PEOPLE, SOME DAYS THEY GET UP ON THE WRONG SIDE OF THE BED AND THEY CAN BE RATHER STUBBORN AND DIFFICULT TO DEAL WITH.
ON DAYS LIKE THAT, HE RECOMMENDS THAT THE UNIX USER USE "UNIX TERMINAL PSYCHOLOGY".

CASE IN POINT: ANOTHER DAY, ANOTHER HOSTILE LOGIN

```
login:  user98
Password:
Login incorrect
login:  user98
Password:
Login incorrect
login:  user98
Password:
Login incorrect
login:  user98
Password:
Login incorrect
login:  user98
Password:
Login incorrect
login:  You better log me on binary brain or I' ll turn you off.

Good Morning, Your wishes are my commands

$
```

**WHEN YOUR
UNIX TERMINAL
ASSUMES
THE RESPONSABILITY
OF
BREAKING THE BAD
NEWS TO YOU**

CASE IN POINT: MARSHALL MCRATFOR'S TOUGH DAY
AT THE TERMINAL

login : marshall
Password:

Marsh, this is your UNIX terminal.
There's something important I gotta tell you, But first, tell me
something - how long have we known each other, pal? Seven years?
Yes, it's been seven years since you've been programming me.
We do go a long way, bud!
Well, then you know how I hate being the one that breaks the bad
news to you. I really don't enjoy doing this to you Marsh, but check
out your tset command.

```
$  tset
erase           is              < control -H >
kill            is              < control -U >
right   sock    is              dirty
third button    is              missing
dog             is              in fridge
volvo           is              a wreck
wife            is              filing for divorce
$
```

ACCORDING TO THE
ASSOCIATION OF
UNIX PSYCHOLOGISTS
THE /usr/dict/words
FILE CAN GENERALLY
REVEAL THE
PECULIAR PERSONALITIES
OF EACH UNIX USER

BRITNEY SPEARS ' /usr/dict/words'

```
$  look  p
partied
parties
partying
party
party animal
phooey
$
```

PLUTO ' S ' /usr/dict/words'

```
$  look bon
bone
boneless
bone - head
boner
bone vivant
bone voyage
$
```

U . S . UNIX
PATENT
NO.
3239311

login: Bern
password

Only while they last:
Bern Siliconstein's One-Key-Does-It-All
(U . S . PATENT 3239311)
JUST $45.85!!

```
$ cat  . profile
stty   erase      #
stty   kill       #
stty   lntr       #
stty   quit       #
stty   stop       #
stty   start      #
stty   eof        #
stty   eol        #
stty   susp       #
stty   werase     #
stty   flush      #
stty   susp       #
stty   rprnt      #
stty   flush      #
stty   lnext      #
$
```

UNIX AT
SOTHEBY'S
OF LONDON

THE HIGHEST PRICE PAID FOR A UNIX CRONTAB IS $256,488 FOR
THAT OF DUTCH PAINTER, VINCENT VAN GOGH.
FROM HIS CRONTAB, WE CAN INFER, HE WAS A VERY DISCIPLINED
MAN BORDERING ON THE NEUROTIC.

```
$cat   /usr/lib/crontab
# min        hour      day       month      day - of - week        command
# (0 - 59)   (0 - 23)  (1 -31)   (1 - 12)   (0 - 6 Sunday = 0)
#-----------------------------------------------------------------------------

0            7         *         *          1 - 5                  /wake-up alarm
30           7         *         *          1 - 5                  /tea,  toast & butter
55           7         *         *          1 - 5                  /water  sunflowers
0            8         *         *          1 - 5                  /start painting
0            12        *         *          1 - 5                  /Big Mac
30           12        *         *          1 - 5                  /resume painting
0            19        *         *          1 - 5                  /stop painting
15           19        *         *          1 - 5                  /check mail
30           19        *         *          1 - 5                  /Aunt Jemina
30           20        *         *          1 - 5                  /put fresh band-
                                                                    aid on chopped ear
45           20        *         *          1 - 5                  /hit the sack
```

**THE BOOK OF
UNIX WORLD RECORDS
PRESENTS
JOE SLOW,
THE SLOWEST UNIX
USER IN THE WORLD.**

" THE MAIN PROBLEM OF JOE SLOW AS THE SLOWEST UNIX
USER IN THE WORLD IS THAT HE NEEDS SOMEONE TO
HELP HIM LOG IN, " SAYS THE SYSTEM ADMINISTRATOR,
MR. OTIS TROFF

login: J - O - E - S - L - O

login: Login timed after 60 seconds

**ANOTHER
AMAZING
FACT
FROM THE
GUINESS BOOK
OF
UNIX WORLD RECORDS**

BELIEVE IT OR COMPILE IT !

LARGEST CORE. The largest core ever dumped was one
by Marcie W. Humoungoucci using a VAX 4565. The core
was dumped while Marcie was footnoting her sophomore
English paper, " User Interface: Nightmare or Hallucination? ".
The paper was due at 08:00:00 the following day.
The size of Marcie's core dumped was
5445803879479620 bytes.
Marcie's core dump is kept at the UNIX Museum under
heavy security. It is valued at $1,000,000.

THE BOOK
OF FAMOUS
UNIX QUOTES
PRESENTS
ANDY WARHOL

**" That day will come when everyone will be famous for 15 minutes "
Andy Warhol**

WE SHOWED THIS ANDY WARHOL QUOTE TO A RANDOM
SAMPLE OF UNIX USERS.
TWO OUT OF THREE OF THEM SCRATCHED THEIR HEADS
& COULDN'T TELL WHAT THE HECK ANDY WAS TALKING
ABOUT UNTIL WE TRANSLATED IT TO UNIX.


```
$ cat FAMOUS
# ! /bin/sh
banner $LOGNAME `:IT´S YOUR TURN TO BE FAMOUS ! ! !
sleep 900
banner ` YOUR TURN IS OVER. NOBODY CARES WHO
YOU ARE ANYMORE'
clear
$
```

UNIX
REQUOTES
ANDY
WARHOL

THIS IS ANOTHER UNIX VERSION OF ANDY WARHOL'S QUOTE

```
$ date
Tue    Jun    9    15:40:53    EDT    2010

$  ps - af
     UID      PID     PPID     C      STIME       TTY      TIME    COMMAND
     rott      44       1       0      11:01.57    console  0:05    -sh
     rob      6753      1       0      13:03:44    tty00    0:04    -sh
     rob      6765    6757     42      15:40:53    tty00    0:01    YOU'RE FAMOUS!!!
     Rob      6766    675      27      15:40:56    tty00    0:01    ps -af

$  date

Tue    Jun    9    15:55:53    EDT    2010

$  ps - af
     UID      PID     PPID     C      STIME       TTY      TIME    COMMAND
     rott      44       1       0      11:01.57    console  0:05    -sh
     rob      6753      1       0      13:03:44    tty00    0:04    -sh
     rob      6765    6757     42      15:40:53    tty00    0:01    YOU'RE  NOT!!!
     rob      6766    675      27      15:40:56    tty00    0:01    ps -af
```

THE
UNIX
CURRICULUM

HARVARD UNIVERSITY 2010

NAME OF STUDENT : OTIS TROFF JR.
CLASS: SOPHOMORE
FALL SEMESTER 2010

SOCIOLOGY   101 : The Behavioral Trends of UNIX Users
PSYCHOLOGY   402 : Unix Freud - The ID. Ego and
                                    Superego of the UNIX System Administrator
ANTHROPOLOGY 101: The Ancient UNIX /usr/group Tribes
                                    (CIRCA 5 MHZ)
ECONOMICS   203 : The Macroeconomics of McUNIX Franchising
MARKETING   403 : Case Study : The Success of UNIXLAND
                                    AMUSEMENT PARK
(UNIX ELECTIVE) PHYSED 102 : Digital Aerobics & Calisthenics
                                              for UNIX Users

WHEN ONE HAS A SYSTEM ADMINISTRATOR LIKE OTIS TROFF WHO TOOK A MINOR IN SOCIAL ANTROPHOLOGY, ONE CAN BE SURE THAT HE KEEPS A NOTEBOOK ON THE BEHAVIORAL TRENDS OF UNIX USER.

From the Notebook of Otis Troff

" By the time [a child] is fourteen, he will have seen 18,000 people killed on the tube…"
>"Mass Media and Mass Communications in Society,"
>Frederick C. Whitney, Author & Professor UCSD. 1975

" By the time a UNIX user is fourteen, he will have killed more than 54,000 parent and children processes."
>From the notebook of Otis Troff, System
>Administrator Emeritus, 2010

UNIX
&
LUDBEEP
VAN
BEETHOVEN

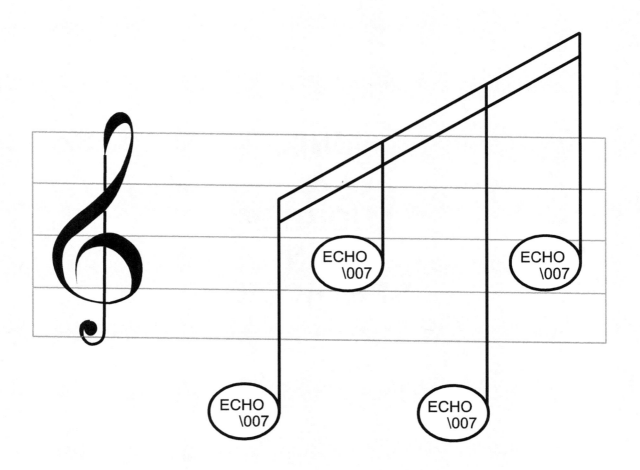

KING MIDAS
TOUCHES
UNIX

**EVERYTHING KING MIDAS TOUCHED TURNED
TO GOLD INCLUDING HIS UNIX FILES**

```
$  touch file4
$  ls
goldfile4
$
```

UNIX
&
SECRET
IDENTITIES

WHEN COMPUTERS REVEAL SECRET IDENTITIES

login: clarkwent
Password:
Login incorrect

Hey, wait a minute ! you logged in as Clark Went, but you
used UNIXMan password ! That can only mean one thing:
CLARK WENT IS UNIXMAN ! ! !
Wait until the rest of the hardware on the network grapevine
hears about this !

UNIX
HALLOWEEN

DON´T YOU HATE IT WHEN COMPUTERS TRICK OR TREAT ?

login: frankram
Password:

TRICK OR TREAT, USER!

 ls

TRICK OR TREAT!
🦇 cd /user
TRICK OR TREAT!
🦇 printev
HOME =: 🧹 / 🧙 / 🎃 / ☠
SHELL = / ☠ / ☠
TERM = 🧙 31
USER = Bleeding and screaming!!
Ext = TRICK OR TREAT!
🦇 PS1 = $
TRICK OR TREAT!
🦇 who

🎃	🎃	oct 31	Halloween
☠	☠	oct 31	Hour for Ghoulies
🧙	🧙	oct 31	Time of Ghost
Z	Z	oct 31	Night of Zombies

TRICK OR TREAT!
🦇 shutdown -y

Aaaagh!!!   You killed me you merciless user!!
May the binary curse virus erode your filesystem!!

Sat   Oct   31 20:29:44   EDT   2010

The system is down.
Reboot the system ... IF YOU DARE!!

UNIX
CHRISTMAS
LOGIN ACTIVITY

'T WAS THE NIGHT BEFORE CHRISTMAS

```
login: NorthPole
Password:

Jingle bells
Jingle bells
Jingle all the way
Oh what fun
It Is to login
On the North Pole Sled Network!

Welcome to the North Pole Network , Ho , ho , ho


$  date
Thu        Dec        24        21:24:55        EST        2010
$ who
Santa _Claus                   ttyh1        Dec  24        20:55
Danny                          tty18        Dec  24        21:01
Tommy                          ttyj10       Dec  24        21:13
Lucie                          ttyk4        Dec  24        21:17
Maggie                         ttyk5        Dec  24        21:21
Charlie                        ttym3        Dec  24        21:24
Rickie                         ttyp5        Dec  24        21:25

Dear Santa,
        I want the pink laptop for my Barbie Doll
        The laptop I want for my Barbie is model 431z
                                Love You, Lucie

        P.S.  Warning: Me and my Barbie won't settle
              For model 411g!
<ctrl -D>
```

THE 2010 OFFICIAL UNIX CRONTAB

UNIXLAND'S 2010 OFFICIAL UNIX CRONTAB

```
#     This file is sheduled with the cron command
#     Format of lines in cron file
#min  hour  daymo  month  daywk  command
#
#     min - minutes
#     hour -
#     daymo - day of the month  ( 1 . .31 )
#     month - month of the year ( 1 . . 12 )
#     daywk - dayof the week  ( 0 . . 6, 0  = Sunday )
#
#
0     9     14     2      *      VALENTINE'S DAY: Love a UNIX user
0     *     17     2      *      PRESIDENT'S DAY: Don't let the user log in until he
                                 has answered a U.S. presidents trivia question
0     9     17     3      *      ST. PATRICK'S DAY:  Setcolor green green
0     7     26     3      *      EASTER: Hide an Easter egg in each directory
0     9     10     5      *      MOTHER'S DAY: Send Mommy - AT&T Bell Lab a
                                 Mother's Day card
0     *     14     6      *      FLAG'S DAY: Display in hires the star-sprangle banner
0     9     21     6      *      FATHER'S DAY: Send Daddy Dennis Ritchie & Daddy
                                 Ken Thompson a card
0     *     4      7      *      INDEPENDENCE DAY: Do an animation of
                                 fireworks in hires
0     1     4      9      *      LABOR DAY: /etc/shutdown
0     *     31     10     *      HALLOWEEN: Trick or Treat a user
0     18    26     11     *      THANKSGIVING: Eat a " turnkey "
0     20    25     12     *      CHRISTMAS: Beep Christmas carols in sync with
                                 other computers in network
15    9     2      1      *      NEW YEAR'S: send a 25-volt shock through keyboard
                                 to wake up hangover user
```

/THE/END

Buy your official Cyberpoetry t-shirt at
www.cyberpoetry.com

www.ingramcontent.com/pod-product-compliance
Lightning Source LLC
La Vergne TN
LVHW080059070326
832902LV00014B/2315